The
Golden Temple

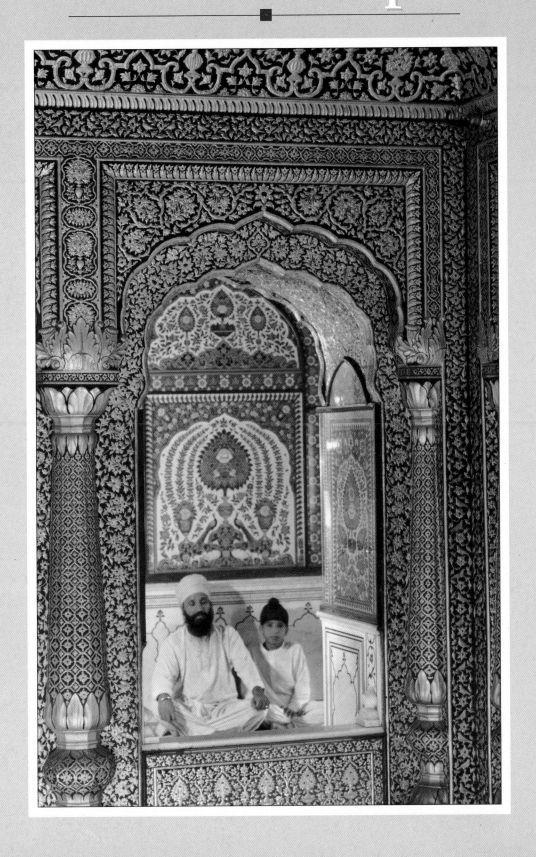

The Golden Temple

Text by Mohinder Singh
Photographs by Sondeep Shankar

UBS PUBLISHERS' DISTRIBUTORS LTD.

IN ASSOCIATION WITH

NATIONAL INSTITUTE OF PANJAB STUDIES

NATIONAL INSTITUTE OF PANJAB STUDIES, NEW DELHI

Advisory Committee:

Prof. Mulk Raj Anand
Prof. Amrik Singh
Prof. Bipan Chandra
Dr. J.S. Neki
Prof. B.N. Goswamy

Series Editor: Dr. Mohinder Singh
Research Associate: Rishi Singh

UBS PUBLISHERS' DISTRIBUTORS LTD.

5 Ansari Road, New Delhi-110 002
Phones: 3273601, 3266646 • Cable: ALLBOOKS • Fax: 3276593, 3274261
E-mail: ubspd@gobookshopping.com • Website: www.gobookshopping.com

10 First Main Road, Gandhi Nagar, Bangalore-560 009
Phones: 2263901, 2263902, 2253903 • Cable: ALLBOOKS
Fax: 2263904 • E-mail: ubspd.bng@bgl.vsnl.net.in

6, Sivaganga Road, Nungambakkam, Chennai-600 034
Phones: 8276355, 8270189 • Cable: UBSIPUB • Fax: 8278920
E-mail: ubspd.che@md4.vsnl.net.in

8/1-B, Chowringhee Lane, Kolkata-700 016
Phones: 2441821, 2442910, 2449473 • Cable: UBSIPUBS
Fax: 2450027 • E-mail: ubspdcal@cal.vsnl.net.in

5 A, Rajendra Nagar, Patna-800 016
Phones: 672856, 673973, 686170 • Cable: UBSPUB • Fax: 686169
E-mail: ubspdpat@dte2.vsnl.net.in

80, Noronha Road, Cantonment, Kanpur-208 004
Phones: 369124, 362665, 357488 • Fax: 315122
E-mail: ubsknp@sancharnet.in

Distributors for Western India:
M/s Preface Books
Unit No. 223 (2nd floor), Cama Industrial Estate,
Sun Mill Compound, Lower Parel (W), Mumbai-400 013
Phone: 022-4988054 • Telefax: 022-4988048 • E-mail: Preface@vsnl.com

Overseas Contact:
475 North Circular Road, Neasden, London NW2 7QG, U.K.
Tele: (020) 8450-8667 • Fax: (020) 8452 6612 Attn: UBS

© National Institute of Panjab Studies

First Published 2002
First Reprint 2002

Cover & Book Design: Dushyant Parasher

Processed and Printed by
Ajanta Offset & Packagings Ltd., New Delhi

Cover
The Golden Temple

Half title page
Interior of the Golden Temple elaborately decorated with painted and gilded designs
Photograph © Hardev Singh

Title spread
A panoramic view of the Golden Temple, the Akal Takhat, the sacred tank and the clock tower
Photograph © Ashok Dilwali

Foreword

The National Institute of Panjab Studies was established in 1990 to promote research on different aspects of Panjabi life and letters. It was subsequently recognised by the Panjab University, Chandigarh, as an advanced centre of learning. Apart from promoting research, the Institute has also been organising lectures, seminars and conferences. Some conferences were also organised in collaboration with other institutions such as the Department of Multicultural Education, University of London, Department of South Asian Studies, University of Michigan, Ann Arbor and the Centre for Global Studies, University of California, Santa Barbara. To mark fifty years of India's independence, the Institute organised an international seminar on 'Partition in Retrospect' in collaboration with the India International Centre, New Delhi.

In connection with the tercentenary of the Khalsa in 1999, the Institute took up a major research project of locating and cataloguing relics which are popularly associated with the Sikh gurus and other historical personalities. Our research team led by the Director of the Institute, visited various parts of India and Pakistan, and located and listed a number of valuable relics. During their field work our team located some very precious relics such as the *chola* of Guru Nanak, the *chola* of Guru Hargobind, *chola*, *dastar* and other relics of Guru Gobind Singh and Mata Sahib Kaur, sword-belt, *godri* and flag of Maharaja Ranjit Singh. Our team was able to take pictures of these and other precious relics and record popular evidence connected with these objects. The team also discovered some rare *Guru Granth Birs*, *hukamnamas* and other historical documents and coins issued by Banda Singh Bahadur, Sikh chiefs, Maharaja Ranjit Singh and his generals.

With a view to sharing the results of our research with the larger audience and creating awareness for proper preservation of the endangered heritage of Panjab and conservation of the valuable relics, the Institute has decided to bring out a series of pictorial books under the 'Panjab Heritage Series'.

The Institute would like to record its gratitude to the Department of Culture, Government of India, for its initial grant for preparing a 'Catalogue of the Sikh Relics', to the Government of the National Capital of Delhi and the Delhi Sikh Gurdwara Management Committee for their financial support for publication of these books and to various institutions and individuals for allowing the Institute's team access to their rich collections. I would also like to thank my colleagues on the Governing Council and staff of the Institute without whose active cooperation it would not have been possible to bring out these volumes.

Manmohan Singh

President
National Institute of Panjab Studies
Bhai Vir Singh Marg
New Delhi - 110 001

Acknowledgements

The National Institute of Panjab Studies acknowledges its gratitude to the following for their contribution to the Panjab Heritage Series:

- The National Museum, New Delhi
- The National Archives of India, New Delhi
- The Panjab State Archives and the Panjab State Museum, Chandigarh, Patiala and Amritsar
- The Shiromani Gurdwara Prabandhak Committee, Amritsar, for permitting us to take photographs of the relics in the Toshakhana of the Golden Temple and sacred weapons at the Akal Takhat, Amritsar, Takhat Sri Kesgarh Sahib, Anandpur, Takhat Damdama Sahib, Talwandi Sabo
- Takhat Sri Patna Sahib, Bihar
- Takhat Sri Hazoor Sahib, Nanded
- The Sikh Regimental Centre, Ramgarh
- Capt. Amarinder Singh, New Moti Bagh Palace, Patiala
- The Bagrian family at Quila Bagrian
- The Sangha family of Drolli Bhai Ki
- Family of Mai Desan, Chak Fateh Singhwala
- Family of Bhai Rupa, Village Bhai Rupa, Dist. Bhatinda
- Family of Bhai Dalla, Talwandi Sabo, Dist. Bhatinda
- Mrs. Jyoti Rai, American Numismatic Society
- Dr. Jean Marie Lafont, French Embassy, New Delhi
- Gurdwara Sri Hemkunt Sahib Management Trust, Kanpur
- S. Bhajan Singh, Chairman, Singapore Sikh Education Foundation
- Department of Archeology and Museums, Government of Pakistan, for permission to take photographs of relics of Maharaja Ranjit Singh and his family in Princess Bamba collection, Lahore Fort Museum, Lahore
- Hardev Singh, Raghu Rai, Ashok Dilwali, Gurmeet Thukral, Manohar Singh, Satpal Danish and Dushyant Parasher for allowing to use their pictures
- Dr S S Bhugra, Dr Susan Stronge, J D Dewan, Mrs Mohinder Singh, Ranjit Kaur and Ashwani Kumar for their input to the project
- Faqir Syed Saif-ud-Din, Fakir Khana Museum, Lahore
- Syed Afzal Haidar, Lahore
- The Victoria & Albert Museum, London.

Facing page
Details of a panel engraved in gold depicting Guru Nanak flanked by his companions– Bala and Mardana

Spread on pages 8-9
An early engraving of the Golden Temple

Spread on pages 10-11
Devotees in the parikarma *of the Temple*

Spread on pages 12-13
An aerial view of the Golden Temple, the sacred tank and adjoining buildings
Photograph © Manohar Singh

Page 14
Most newly weds begin their married lives after offering prayers at the Golden Temple

Page 15
The Holy Book installed inside the sanctum sanctorum under beautifully embroidered velvet canopy and interiors inlaid with floral patterns

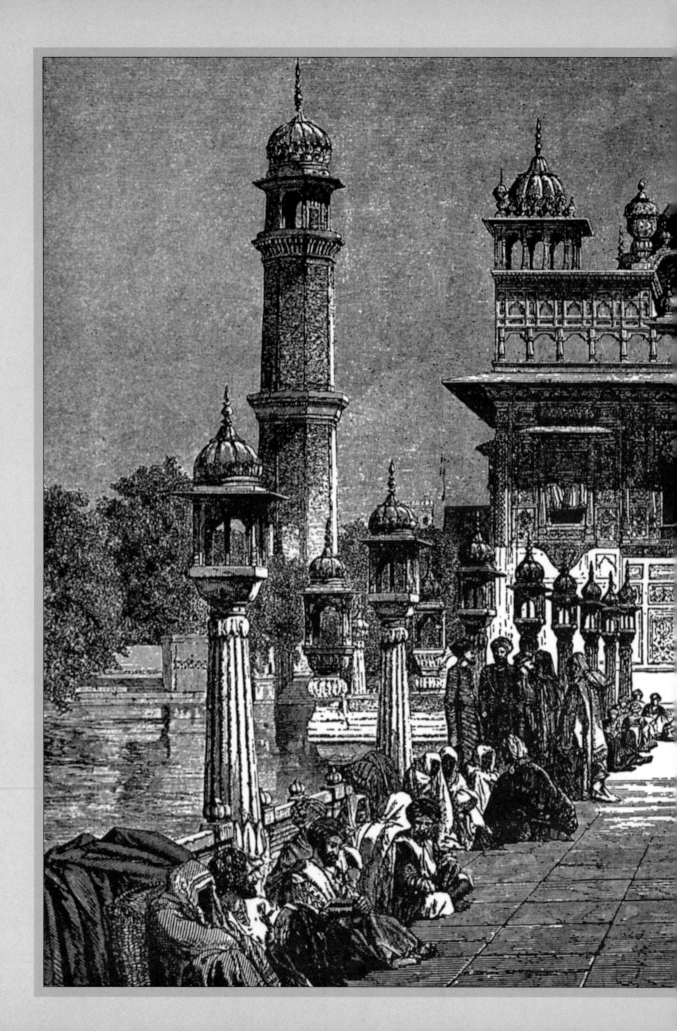

Above: A devotee lost in meditation in the precincts of the Golden Temple

Left: Devotees taking amrit *from Har ki Pauri*
Photograph © Raghu Rai

Since its establishment in AD 1589, Harimandir, popularly known as the Golden Temple, has been a living symbol of spiritual and historical traditions of the Sikhs. It is much more to the Sikhs than a mere place of worship. The Sikhs have their roots in the immortal water of the sacred tank surrounding the temple. According to popular accounts, when contemporary Emperor Akbar was returning to his capital after a military campaign, he halted at Goindwal to have an audience with the third Guru, Amar Das. The emperor was so much impressed by the guru's teachings of equality and the institution of *langar* that he made a gift of land on which the guru's successor, Guru Ram Das, built the town of Ramdaspur, later known as Amritsar. There are other accounts, which mention that the town was established on a piece of land purchased by Guru Ram Das from the landlords of village Tung, district Jhabal.

It was the fifth Guru, Arjan Dev, who widened the pool of nectar existing on the land and made the tank *pucca*. He also provided stairs on all the four sides of the tank. In consultation with Baba Buddha, the revered Sikh saint, the guru decided to build a temple in the centre of the sacred pool and called it Harimandir, the Abode of God. At the guru's request, a Muslim saint of Lahore, Mian Mir, laid the foundation of the Harimandir in AD 1588. The guru purposely provided four doors, one in each direction, signifying its accessibility to people from all the four directions, irrespective of caste and creed. Construction of the Harimandir and the sacred tank witnessed the first ever *kar-seva* performed by the Sikhs under the overall supervision of Guru Arjan Dev assisted by two devout Sikh leaders, Bhai Gurdas and Baba Buddha. The *ber* tree, popularly known as *lachiber*, near the Darshani Deohdi, under which the guru sat while overseeing the construction stands a witness to the great project conceived and completed by the guru.

Because of constant flow of cash contributions made by the followers of the guru from different parts of the country, construction work was carried out with great speed and enthusiasm. While the construction work was on, devotees from far and near visited the place to offer voluntary service in this

unique project. Some of the leading chiefs of nearby villages also made cash contribution for the construction of the temple. Along with construction of the temple, the guru also paid attention to the development of the town. New markets were opened and people from nearby areas were encouraged to start business there. Persons belonging to different castes and professions were encouraged to settle in the vicinity of the temple in order to provide a cosmopolitan and egalitarian character to the city in keeping with the teachings of the Sikh faith.

Compilation of the *Adi Granth*

While the hymns of Guru Nanak and his successors, Angad Dev, Amar Das and Ram Das, were already in circulation in some form or the other, Guru Arjan Dev thought it proper to prepare an anthology of these hymns. It was intended that the hymns could become the focal point for the emerging community of the followers. For this purpose Guru Arjan Dev acquired the hymns from Baba Mohan, son of the third Guru, Amar Das, and also invited compositions from various other

Left: Golden Temple in AD 1833. Photograph by Lance Dane of an engraving by W. Carpenter Junior

Below: Dargah of the Sufi Saint Mian Mir in Lahore. According to popular tradition, the foundation stone of the Harimandir was laid by Mian Mir.

Hindu *bhaktas* and Muslim saints. After having collected the required material, Guru Arjan Dev began to dictate the hymns to Bhai Gurdas at a place called Ramsar not very far from the Harimandir.

The hymns in the *Guru Granth* are not arranged author-wise but are divided into musical modes indicating how they should be sung. The scripture has been standardised to a format of 1,438 pages. It contains nearly 6,000 hymns, the largest number being those of the fifth Guru, Arjan Dev, at 2,218, followed by those of Guru Nanak (974), Guru Amar Das (907), Guru Ram Das (679), Guru Tegh Bahadur (115) and Guru Angad

Above: When the fifth Guru, Arjan Dev, decided to compile the Adi Granth, *Bhai Gurdas (AD 1551-1636) assisted the guru by inscribing the Holy Book. He also wrote poetry in the form of* Varan, *which is considered to be the basic source for understanding Sikh religion.*

Right: Gurdwara Ramsar marks the place where the fifth Guru, Arjan Dev, compiled the Holy Book.

Dev (62). Besides the hymns of the gurus, those of Hindu *bhaktas* and Muslim saints belonging to different areas have also been included. The poetic compositions of Jaidev of Bengal, Namdev, Trilochan and Parmanand of Maharashtra, Sadhna of Sindh, Bene, Rama Nand, Kabir and Ravidas from Uttar Pradesh, and the famous Sufi Saint Sheikh Farid from Pak Pattan (now in Pakistan) are included in the Holy Book. The *Guru Granth* is perhaps the only scripture in the world which is an inter-faith work both in terms of its contents and message.

Installation of the *Adi Granth* in the Golden Temple

After the compilation of the *Adi Granth* in AD 1604, the fifth guru appointed Baba Buddha, the most revered Sikh of the time, as the first *granthi* of the temple. According to contemporary sources, the *Holy Granth* wrapped in silk *rumalas* was brought to the sanctum sanctorum in a palanquin carried by the devout Sikhs with Guru Arjan Dev waving the *chavar* as a mark of respect and barefooted devotees following in a procession. The *Holy Granth* was placed in the sanctum sanctorum on a cot with Baba Buddha in attendance and the congregation sitting all around with great devotion. Guru Arjan then asked Baba Buddha to open the *Granth* at random and read out a hymn to the assembled congregation.

The guru also introduced the practice of *kirtan*. This perhaps is the only Sikh shrine where the *Guru Granth* is placed on a cot on the floor and not a high wooden or cemented pedestal as can be seen in most of other Sikh shrines. The Golden Temple has a few other unique features, one of them being that no *katha* or lectures are delivered in the sanctum sanctorum. To discuss temporal affairs, the sixth Guru, Hargobind, built the Akal Takhat just opposite the Darshani Deohdi, the main entrance to the causeway leading to the sanctum. Even today, every evening the Holy Book is closed after due ceremonies and taken to a room called Kotha Sahib where Guru Arjan resided. While the *Holy Granth* was placed for rest on a cot, the guru himself slept on the floor as a mark of respect. Every morning the Holy Book was carried to the sanctum sanctorum

Above: Bura Randhawa (AD 1506-1631), popularly known as Baba Buddha, was the most revered figure of early Sikhism. He was contemporary of Guru Nanak and had the unique privilege of anointing five gurus—Angad, Amardas, Ramdas, Arjan and Hargobind. Along with Guru Arjan Dev, he supervised the construction of the Golden Temple and was appointed its first granthi *after the Holy Book was installed in the sanctum sanctorum in AD 1604.*

Page 22: Mool Mantra *on the first folio of the original copy of the* Adi Granth
This *bir of* Adi Granth *is preserved with descendants of the guru at Kartarpur, Panjab. Courtesy: Dr Pashaura Singh*

Page 23: Inside the Harimandir—a water colour by William Carpenter, 1854 Courtesy: Victoria and Albert Museum, London

in a palanquin in procession with the devotees singing hymns and waving the fly-whisk.

It is important to mention that the Sikhs do not worship any idol or human beings. Since the *Guru Granth* itself has the status of the guru, it occupies a central place in the Sikh gurdwara. It is installed on a platform with a canopy covering it as a mark of respect while an attendant standing behind the *granthi* fans it with a fly-whisk. On entering the gurdwara, the devotees prostrate before the Holy Book and make a ceremonial offering of money and flowers as a mark of respect. Then they sit, with heads covered, in a quiet posture to listen either to the hymns being recited by the *granthi*, or to the *kirtan* recited by musicians known as *ragis*.

Daily Routine at the Golden Temple

The routine set by the fifth guru has continued to be the guiding spirit in the Golden Temple with a few interruptions— first when the temple was twice destroyed by the Afghan invaders and more recently during the tragic events of 1984. Following is the daily routine in the temple.

Opening of the Entrance Doors

The Golden Temple remains open practically the whole day except for a short interval of four hours during the night— 12.00 p.m. to 4.00 a.m.—when the Holy Book is put to rest at Kotha Sahib. The doors of the Darshani Deohdi, which are closed at 11:00 p.m., reopen at 3:00 a.m. When the sanctum sanctorum remains closed, a few volunteers stay inside for washing and cleaning the temple, dusting and changing the floor sheets. The washing is done with milk diluted with water taken from the Har-ki-Pauri. The floor is then wiped with towels. The outer *parikarma* is also washed with water and wiped. While the volunteers perform this service of cleaning the sanctum sanctorum and the *parikarma*, non-stop singing of hymns continues outside. One can hear the hymns either being recited by the *ragi jathas* or sung by the volunteers all the twenty-four hours in the sacred premises. Also non-stop reading of the Holy Scripture continues on the upper storey of the Golden Temple.

Left above: During the ambrosial hour, the Holy Book is carried by the devotees in a palanquin from Kotha Sahib to the sanctum sanctorum.

Left below: In the evening, the Holy Book is taken back to Kotha Sahib after due ceremonies.

Below: A devotee paying obeisance

Following page: Sikh tradition lays great importance on taking bath early in the morning. Devotees who visit the Golden Temple make it a point to have a dip in the sacred tank before paying obeisance in the sanctum sanctorum.

Page 27: Before the sunset rehras, *the evening prayer, is offered daily at the temple.*

Double spread pages 28-29: Harimandir is constructed in the midst of the sacred tank and is the source of inspiration and spiritual bliss for the devotees across the world.

Double spread pages 30-31: After the completion of kar-seva *of fresh gold plating in 1999, the temple shines in the midst of the sacred tank and the adjoining buildings.*
Photograph © Manohar Singh

Left: Nihangs, *knight-errants of Guru Gobind Singh, listening to the holy hymns*
Photograph © Manohar Singh

Right: Enthusiastic devotees entering the sanctum sanctorum

Below: Baba Deep Singh, the legendary Sikh hero, proved the efficacy of ardas. *After being seriously injured during a battle at Ram Rauni, he continued fighting the enemy till he reached the precincts of the Golden Temple, where he breathed his last after liberating the holy shrine. Below is the memorial in the* parikarma *depicting heroic deed of Baba Deep Singh.*

Following page: A view of the Golden Temple through the Darshani Deohdi

Page 35: Devotees offering prayers inside the Golden Temple

Double spread pages 36-37: A priest reading from the hand-written bir of Guru Granth Sahib *on the first floor of the Golden Temple*

Pages 38 and 39: Details of the inlay work and floral patterns inside the Golden Temple

Pages 40 and 41: Devotees on the first floor either sit in quite meditation or read from the prayer books.

Above: Ath Sath Tirath *marks the place where, sitting under the* ber *tree, Guru Arjan Dev supervised the construction of the sacred tank.*

Right: Devotees listening to the kirtan

Left above: Baba Budha's beri *is located on the northern side of the* parikrama *and marks the site from where the Baba looked after the construction work of the Golden Temple.*

Left below: Complete surrender to the Almighty is one of the basic principles of Sikh faith.

Right: The Golden Temple, with doors provided in four directions of the sanctum sanctorum, is open to devotees of all colours and creeds.

Below: Devotees taking amrit *from Har-ki-pauri*

Facing page: Beautifully decked up young Panj Piaras *in the Golden Temple precincts*

Page 46: Conspicuous by their headgear, double-edged swords and dark blue and saffron yellow garments, the Nihangs *(literally dragoons) are members of an order instituted by the tenth guru. Earlier they were also called Akalis (deathless or immortal) and were willing to die for the protection of their faith and places of worship.*

Page 47 above: Langar, serving free food prepared in community kitchen attached to the gurdwara, has been an important feature of Sikh faith from its inception. In this painting by Bodhraj, Akbar, the Mughal Emperor of India, is seen taking food in the langar along with his nobles and servants during his visit to the third guru.

Page 47 below: Serving drinking water is an important aspect of the concept of seva. *This is a picture of* piao *in the* parikarma *of the temple.*

Double spread pages 48-49: After every ceremony, karah prashad, *the sweet sacrament, is distributed to the congregation in keeping with Sikh spirit of service and equality.*

Kirtan

After the opening of the doors and installation of the *Guru Granth* in the sanctum sanctorum, non-stop *kirtan* performed by a chain of *ragi jathas* continues. Of late, early morning kirtan is relayed on the radio and also shown on various television networks for the benefit of the devotees living in different parts of the world. The *kirtan* starts one hour after the opening of the gates in the morning and is followed by recitation from *Asa Di Var*, and then the *Guru Granth* is installed. At 12 noon the *ragis* recite *Anand Sahib* while *Charan Kamal Arti* is performed at 3 p.m. From 5 p.m. to 6:15 p.m. the *ragis* recite *Sodar*, and from 6:45 p.m. to 8:00 p.m. they perform *arti* through *kirtan*. After the evening prayer, *kirtan* is resumed and it goes on till 9:45 p.m. With this ends the devotional singing for the day when, after due ceremonies, the *Guru Granth* is taken back to Kotha Sahib for rest during the night.

Left: Sangat *listening to* kirtan *in the holy precinct.*

Below: Singh Sahib Yogi Harbhajan Singh Khalsa, popularly known as Yogiji, has been greatly instrumental in encouraging a vast number of Americans to embrace Sikh religion. In the picture, Yogi Harbhajan Singh and his followers are paying obeisance in the sanctum sanctorum.

Akal Takhat

Akal Takhat, the Throne of the Immortal, is situated adjacent to the main entrance of the Harimandir. Guru Hargobind, the sixth Guru, laid the foundation of the Akal Takhat. Baba Buddha and Bhai Gurdas completed the work of its construction. Whereas the Harimandir stands for spiritual guidance, the Akal Takhat stands as a symbol of temporal authority of the Sikh religion. It is here that all important issues affecting the Sikh community are discussed and major decisions taken. *Hukamnamas* to the Sikhs all over the world are also issued from the Akal Takhat. To infuse martial spirit among the followers, the guru appointed some bards who would sing heroic ballads from the Sikh history. This tradition continues till date.

Left: To take vital decisions concerning the Sikh panth, Sarbat Khalsa is organised at Akal Takhat. Picture shows the recent Sarbat Khalsa held at the Akal Takhat
Photograph © Raghu Rai

Below: Historic weapons belonging to the gurus are preserved in the Akal Takhat. They are displayed daily after the evening service.

Following double spread: A rare painting of the Akal Takhat in water colour painted by William Simpson in 1860
Courtesy: Victoria and Albert Museum, London

Double spread pages 56-57: A majestic view of the Akal Takhat with two Nishan Sahibs *flying high, symbolising spiritual and temporal authority of the Sikh faith*

53

Left: Dhadi Jatha, *outside the Akal Takhat, singing ballads from the Sikh tradition*
Photograph © Manohar Singh

Below: Sacred weapons belonging to the gurus and Baba Deep Singh displayed at the Akal Takhat

*Right: Priest of the Akal Takhat displaying the two historic swords—*Miri *and* Piri—*worn by the sixth Guru*

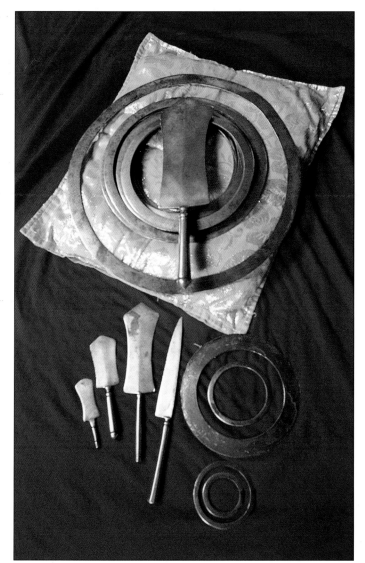

59

During the seventh invasion of Panjab by Ahmad Shah Abdali, the Harimandir and the Akal Takhat were levelled to the ground. As soon as the Afghans left the soil of Amritsar, the Sikhs reconstructed the two. During Maharaja Ranjit Singh's rule (1799-1839), the Akal Takhat was beautified. Hari Singh Nalwa, the famous General of the Maharaja, generously donated for the gold plating of the dome of Akal Takhat. In recent history, the Akal Takhat was destroyed during Operation Blue Star in 1984 and was later rebuilt by the Sikh community through *kar-seva*. Sacred relics are preserved in the Akal Takhat which are shown to the *sangat* daily after the evening service. The well known Miri and Piri swords of Guru Hargobind are also displayed here. The Akal Takhat stands as a symbol of the Sikh spirit of resilience and ascendancy, glory and grandeur.

Management of the Golden Temple

Guru Arjan himself looked after the management of the Golden Temple assisted by two devout Sikhs, Bhai Gurdas and Baba Buddha. After the execution of the guru in AD 1604 and with his son and successor, Guru Hargobind, shifting from Amritsar to Kiratpur, the management and control of the temple passed into the hands of the *masands*. Taking advantage of the situation these *masands* aligned themselves with the enemies of the gurus. Sodhi Meharban, son of Prithi Chand, elder brother of Guru Arjan, managed to take control of the Golden Temple. His son, Sodhi Harji, converted the Harimandir into his personal fiefdom and controlled the shrine for nearly five decades. He became so bold that when Guru Tegh Bahadur, the ninth Guru, wanted to pay obeisance at the sanctum sanctorum, on his instructions, the *masands* slammed the doors on the guru. After taking a dip in the holy tank, the guru halted at a raised platform under a *ber* tree beneath the Akal Bunga. Noticing that the *masands* were unwilling to relent, the guru quietly left the place without being able to pay his homage at the sanctum sanctorum. After halting in a nearby village of Walla Verka, the guru returned to Batala and then shifted to Makhowal where he established a new town, which later became famous as Anandpur. However, after the death of Sodhi Harji, there

Left above: Cupolas and chhatris *on the top of the Golden Temple are fine specimens of art work and gold-plating done by the artisans*

Left below: Dr Inderjit Kaur addressing the students of the Miri-Piri Academy

Below: Because of his life-long dedication to the cause of mentally challenged, Bhagat Puran Singh (1904-1992), became a legend in recent Sikh history. In the photograph one can see him sitting outside the main entrance of the Golden Temple writing and distributing pamphlets on Sikh religion and environmental issues.

61

emerged a serious dispute among his three sons over the control of the Golden Temple. As a result of the conflict, the Minas, followers of Sodhi Harji, got divided and their hold over Golden Temple was greatly weakened.

After the creation of the Khalsa in AD 1699, Guru Gobind Singh paid attention to the management of the Golden Temple. He deputed his trusted childhood friend, Bhai Mani Singh, to take charge of the management of the temple and to carry on the much needed improvements. The guru also issued *hukamnamas* to the Sikhs to assist Bhai Mani Singh in his new assignment. On reaching Amritsar, Bhai Mani Singh and his associates restored all the traditional ceremonies.

However, after the death of Guru Gobind Singh in AD 1708 and persecution of the Sikhs during Banda Singh Bahadur's

Below: To liberate the Golden Temple and other historic Sikh shrines from the control of hereditary mahants, *the Sikhs launched struggle for reform known as the Akali Movement (1920-25). Akali leaders are seen addressing the volunteers outside the Hall Gate, Amritsar.*
Courtesy: Sir George Dunnett, London

leadership, the management of the Golden Temple suffered a serious setback. When most of the Sikhs retired to the jungles or other hideouts, management of the Golden Temple and other historic gurdwaras passed into the hands of the *Udasis*. While they did a great service in keeping the torch of the Sikh faith alive during the period of persecution of the Sikhs, with the passage of time there followed a phase of degeneration. As a result, a section of the Sikhs, called Akali reformers, had to launch a movement of reform for the management of the Golden Temple and the other historic Sikh shrines popularly known as the Akali Movement (1920-25).

Beautification of the Golden Temple

Embellishment of the Harimandir was done a number of times but never the way the artisans commissioned by Maharaja Ranjit Singh did it. The Maharaja got the shrine redecorated with beautiful inlay and floral work. He invited artisans and painters from far and near so that the shrine became a gem floating in the 'Tank of Immortality'. He donated rupees five lakh at the commencement of the *kar-seva* in AD1803.

Below: An Akali jatha *marching towards Guru ka Bagh*
Courtesy: Sir George Dunnett, London

Following double spread: The grandeur of the artwork on the ceiling of the Darshani Deohdi

Double spread pages 66-67: Tranquillity permeates the atmosphere in the Golden Temple precincts at dawn and dusk.

Double spread pages 68-69: Details of the artwork on gold panels of the Darshani Deohdi

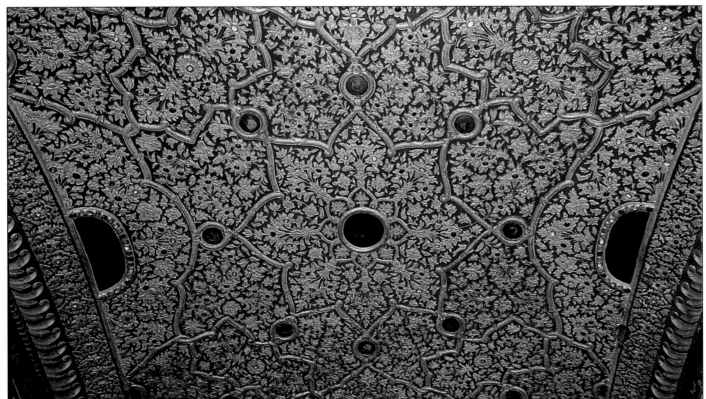

Pages 70-73: As a result of patronage of Maharaja Ranjit Singh, Harimandir was gold-plated and beautified. The interior of the Golden Temple provides one of the best specimens of mirror work of different shapes and sizes, frescos and murals on the side walls. The inlaid marble panels beautifully depict flora and fauna on the exterior walls of the temple with kiosks, chhatris and cupolas, inverted lotus base being the most conspicuous.

The inscription to commemorate this act can be seen at the main entrance.

On the ground floor, the *Guru Granth* is placed under a decorated canopy studded with jewels. The floral decoration work was accomplished by Muslim artisans from Chiniot (now in Pakistan). On the first floor is the Sheesh Mahal or the 'Hall of Mirrors', a small square pavilion, surmounted by a low-fluted golden dome and lined at its base with a number of smaller domes. It was here that Guru Arjan Dev used to sit in meditation. Mirrors and pieces of glass are of different shapes and sizes. This work is known as *jaratkari* technique.

The walls of the two lower storeys, forming parapets, terminate with several rounded pinnacles. There are four *chhatris* or kiosks at the corners. The combination of dozens of large and medium domes of gilded copper creates a dazzling effect, enhanced further by the reflection in the water below. The arches and alcoves of the central hall have been ornamented with floral designs along with the verses from the *Gurbani*. Beautiful borders around the mural paintings enhance the aesthetic aura in the temple. The walls of the Harimandir were inlaid with gold provided by the Maharaja who also contributed much of the white marble. It will not be an exaggeration to say that Maharaja Ranjit Singh contributed a lot in making the Harimandir an object of unique beauty of gold and marble. Hence the place came to be known as *Swaranmandir* or 'The Golden Temple'.

Special Celebrations and Jalao

Though the Golden Temple is frequented by the devotees everyday, there are occasions which are celebrated with great pomp and show when the whole complex is illuminated. These special occasions are the birthdays of Guru Nanak, Guru Ram Das and Guru Gobind Singh. *Guru Granth Sahib* installation day is also celebrated with gaiety and enthusiasm, when precious relics in the *toshakhana* of the Golden Temple located on the top of the Darshani Deohdi are displayed, which is called *jalao*, meaning a show of splendour.

Jalao has a unique history behind it. Right from the inception of the Sikh faith, Sikh gurus and Sikh temples

Below: Entrance to the sanctum sanctorum commemorates the service rendered to the temple by the Maharaja: The Guru was kind enough to allow the privilege of service to Durbar Sahib to his humble servant Maharaja Singh Sahib Ranjit Singh.

Below, far below and right: Maharaja Ranjit Singh presented precious gifts to the Golden Temple as a token of his gratitude. In the pictures are seen two necklaces and a peacock made of sapphire and gilded with diamonds, rubies and pearls

Following double spread: On festive occasions, the Golden Temple and adjoining buildings are profusely illuminated. Diwali in Amritsar is celebrated to mark the return of Guru Hargobind after being released from Gwalior fort by Emperor Jahangir. Photograph © Dushyant Parasher

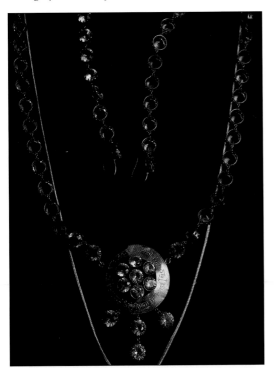

occupied a place of special reverence for the followers of the faith. When the Sikhs gained political supremacy in Panjab, the Sikh chiefs took great pride in offering priceless gifts to the house of the guru. The Golden Temple, being the most prominent of the Sikh shrines, received valuable presents that the Sikhs could ever think of. When Ranjit Singh became the Maharaja of Panjab, he presented to the Golden Temple whatever in his opinion was rare and valuable. There are popular stories which mention that once the Maharaja was presented with a canopy made of pure gold weighing about twenty pounds and studded with emeralds, diamonds, rubies and pearls. The Maharaja found it to be too precious to be used by any human being and offered it to the Golden Temple. On seeing the costly pearls and jewels *sehra* prepared for the marriage of Maharaja's grandson, Kanwar Nau Nihal Singh, the Maharaja felt that this again was too precious to be used by any human being and presented this to the Golden Temple. Some other important relics which are also displayed during the *jalao* are: four golden gates with floral patterns and episodes from gurus' lives engraved upon them, gold *chhatris*, golden frills, golden handfans, golden sword of Maharaja Ranjit Singh studded with jewels and rubies and a fly-whisk made from sandalwood presented by a Muslim saint.

Left: Maharaja Ranjit Singh and other Sikh chiefs not only got the whole temple gold-plated but also provided golden gates with floral patterns and Sikh themes engraved on them.

Below: Details of gold engraving depicting Guru Nanak with Bala and Mardana

Architecture

The original structure of the Golden Temple constructed in the midst of the pool of nectar by the fifth guru was destroyed by the Afghan invader, Ahmad Shah Abdali, in AD 1762. Since the Golden Temple has been the premier Sikh shrine and the main source of inspiration for the Sikhs, they reassembled at Amritsar soon after the retreat of Ahmad Shah Abdali and decided to rebuild the temple. Jassa Singh Ahluwalia, Commander of the Dal Khalsa, gave a call for collecting funds for rebuilding of the Golden Temple. Money thus collected was kept with the bankers of Amritsar and Bhai Des Raj was entrusted with the work of supervision of the construction and collection of the additional funds, if needed, for the project.

Left: Front view of the Golden Temple with reflection in clear water in the sacred tank

Below: Beautiful ornate dome with cupolas and kiosks of the Golden Temple

To assist in work of reconstruction of the Harimandir, several of the Sikh chiefs constructed their own *bungas* around the temple where they could stay while helping in the construction through voluntary labour and donations. Though most of the work in the construction of the temple, the Darshani Deohdi and the brick-lining of the sacred tank was completed by 1784, it was during the reign of Maharaja Ranjit Singh that the temple assumed its present appearance. While Ranjit Singh did not alter the basic design, he commissioned experienced craftsmen and donated liberal funds to transform the temple into a symbol of glory and grandeur of the Sikhs.

In keeping with the Sikh gurus' philosophy of humility and living pure among impurities of life, the Harimandir was intentionally built by the founder at a low level and it floats like a lotus in the pool of nectar. According to Dr. J.S. Neki, the spirit behind the architecture of the Golden Temple is that of spiritual enlightenment and the lotus is the symbol employed to express this spirit. This flower remains crossed with its stem bent down till the sunlight falls on it, when it becomes upright and opens up to blossom. This symbol has been appropriately incorporated in the architectural design of the temple. The main dome of the temple has the form of inverted lotus flower. The same flower is depicted in the arches and designs of the pillars.

According to Dr. K.S. Kang:

The main structure rises from the centre of the sacred pool, 150 metres square, approached by a causeway about 60 meters long. An archway on the western side of the pool opens on to the causeway, bordered with balustrades of fretted marble and, at close intervals, there are standard lamps, their great lattens set upon marble columns. The 52-metre square-based Harimandir, to which the causeway leads, stands on a 20 metre square platform. Its lower parts are of white marble, but the upper parts are covered with plates of gilded copper ('Art and Architecture of the Golden Temple', *Homage to Amritsar*, Marg Publications, Bombay).

Sarovar, or the pool of nectar, has a unique history behind it. Water in the *sarovar* where Dukh Bhanjani Beri is located is a natural reservoir and contains sulphur potentialities with healing properties. To ensure that the tank does not dry up or stagnate, arrangements were made to ensure supply of fresh water through a tributary of river Ravi called Hansli Canal. As a result of the initiative of Mahant Pritam Das and the financial support of the Sikh chiefs and devotees, arrangements were made to dig this special canal for supply of fresh water exclusively to the sacred tank of the Golden Temple.

To keep the water clean, the canal was brick-lined and later covered. Two reservoirs were constructed near the Golden Temple from where the water is siphoned off to the sacred tank which allows the mud and sand particles to settle in the reservoirs. A drain has been provided on all sides of the sacred tank for draining out the dirty water coming from the cleaning of the *parikrama* or rinsing clothes after the holy dip. And most important of all, there is regular outflow of the water of the sacred tank as a result of which there is no algae or growth of aquatic plants.

Kar-seva in the Golden Temple

Kar-seva is voluntary contribution of physical labour in any kind of work for the gurdwara. Guru Arjan performed the first *kar-seva* at Amritsar, which involved not only deepening the holy tank but also brick-lining its banks with steps leading down to the floor. In this labour of love, devout Sikhs like Baba Buddha and others assisted the guru.

Jalao – *display of valuable relics and ornaments in the Toshakhana is arranged on special occasions.*

In the year 1746, the Harimandir was desecrated and the tank was filled with debris by the army of the Abdali invader. The very next year, after regaining control over the shrine, the Sikhs performed *kar-seva*. Jahan Khan, a Mughal commander, once again filled up the sarovar in the year 1757. In the year 1758, *kar-seva* was performed again to cleanse the tank. *Kar-seva* of the tank was also carried out in the year 1842 under the supervision of Bhai Gurmukh Singh.

There was a historic *kar-seva* in the year 1923 during the Gurdwara Reform Movement. Cleaning of the 'Tank of Immortality' was started on the 17 June by the Panj Piaras, who did so by lifting the sledge with gold spades and silver pans after offering prayers, with the Maharaja of Patiala and other Sikh

Below: A rare picture of historic kar-seva *of 1923 in which devout from all walks of life, including Maharaja Bhupinder Singh of Patiala, participated. Courtesy: Satpal Danish*

84

chiefs joining in this labour of love. These spades and pans are preserved in the *toshakhana* along with the other valuable relics. Devotees from far and wide, Hindu, Muslim and Sikh, all joined this historic *kar-seva* in large numbers. In recent times, *kar-seva* was performed in 1985 to cleanse the holy tank after the tragedy of 1984, known as the Operation Blue Star. *Kar-seva*, whenever it takes place, symbolizes the basic tenets of Sikh faith—humility, equality, devotion and spirit of service. To mark the tercentenary of the creation of the Khalsa, the Sikh *sangat* under the supervision of Bhai Mohinder Singh of Guru Nanak Nishkam Sewak Jatha of Birmingham, United Kingdom, completed the *kar-seva* of fresh gold plating of the Golden Temple in AD 1999.

Below: A mammoth gathering of devotees removing silt from the sacred tank during the kar-seva.
Courtesy: Satpal Danish

Following double spread: In the kar-seva *organised by SGPC in 1973 devotees from all over India and abroad enthusiastically participated.*
Courtesy: Satpal Danish

Facilities in the Vicinity

Harimandir has a number of buildings of historical importance around it. The *Langar* hall, adjacent to the shrine, is a place where meals from the community kitchen are prepared by the devotees and served to the visitors. Guru Ram Das Hospital helps the poor and the needy with free medical aid. Guru Ram Das Sarai provides free lodging to the pilgrims. To meet the growing need of the devotees, Guru Nanak Niwas and the Akal Rest House have been added. Next to the *sarai* is the office of the Shiromani Gurdwara Prabandhak Committee (SGPC), a statutory body for the management of historic Sikh shrines. On the first floor of the main entrance is the Central Sikh Museum. It displays rare paintings of the Sikh heritage. It also has a rich collection of antiques, coins, rare documents, manuscripts, old arms and other relics.

*Below: Baba Atal, a water colour by
William Carpenter
Courtesy: Victoria and Albert Museum, London*

*Right: Details of wall paintings from
Baba Atal building*

Right below: The Langar *hall in the
Golden Temple complex*

*Facing page: A major project to beautify the
surroundings of the Golden Temple was taken up by
the Government of Panjab, which led to widening of
roads, provision of lights and creation of green spots.
Photograph © Manohar Singh*

Golden Temple

and Popular Movements

Since its inception, the Golden Temple has been the main source of inspiration for the Sikh community. Among the Sikh shrines it enjoys a unique place. Guru Arjan Dev, the founder, thus describes the glory of the place: "I have seen all places; but there is none other like Thee, for Thou wert established by the Creator-Lord Himself, Who blessed Thee with glory." Unfortunately, the beauty of the place became its bane and it was subjected to repeated invasions during the eighteenth century. Realising the importance of the Harimandir in the Sikh psyche, successive invaders made several attempts to destroy the temple and the sacred tank around it. In April 1709, the Muslim Governor of Lahore set up a police post at Amritsar and sent an army to suppress the Sikhs. Undeterred, the Sikhs continued to throng the Harimandir and made special efforts to take a dip in the sacred tank on festive days like Baisakhi and Diwali. When Zakariya Khan, the Mughal Governor of Lahore, decided to make peace with the Sikhs in 1733 by offering the title of Nawab to their leader Kapur Singh, Harimandir again got into prominence. Two years later when the Mughal governor broke his promise of peace, Harimandir once again became the target of Mughal attacks.

Massa Ranghar, who was appointed *kotwal* of the town in AD 1737, befouled the sacred tank and made the Harimandir a rendezvous for his dancing girls. In keeping with the Sikh spirit, two devout Sikhs—Bhai Sukha Singh and Bhai Mehtab Singh—came out from their hideouts in Rajasthan, entered the Harimandir in disguise, killed Massa Ranghar in broad daylight and rode back to safety carrying the tyrant's head as a trophy.

Since the Harimandir and the sacred tank at Amritsar were the main source of inspiration for the Sikhs, the Afghan invader, Ahmad Shah Abdali, after having attacked Delhi in AD 1757, desecrated the temple and defiled the sacred tank by filling it with waste and entrails of slaughtered cows. However, the Sikhs, led by Baba Deep Singh, the legendary Sikh General, attacked the Afghan soldiers, defeated and captured them and had the

Below: During the fifth centenary of the birth of Guru Nanak Dev, a new university named after the guru was established at Amritsar in 1969.

holy tank cleansed by the captured Afghan soldiers. Five years later when Ahmad Shah Abdali invaded India for the sixth time in AD 1762, the Harimandir again became the subject of attack when he had the sacred shrine blown up with gunpowder. The Sikhs did not allow the spirit of ascendancy to dampen and gathered at Harimandir to celebrate the traditional festival of Diwali. Two years later Jassa Singh Ahluwalia, Commander of the Dal Khalsa, gave a call for collection of funds and the rebuilding of the Harimandir.

With the weakening of the authority of Ahmad Shah Abdali and gradual disintegration of the Mughal empire in India, the Sikhs organised themselves into twelve confederacies (or *misls*) and established their supremacy over the territories conquered by each *misl*. Keeping in mind the central role that the Harimandir played in Sikh history during their turbulent days, the Sikh chiefs paid special attention to rebuilding and beautification of the Harimandir and the Akal Takhat—centre of spiritual and temporal authority of the Sikh *panth*.

The Golden Temple and the Akal Takhat have played a decisive role in Sikh history. It was from the sacred precincts of the Golden Temple that the Sikh gurus issued instructions to the devout Sikhs. After the introduction of the system of *daswandh*, Sikh leaders put in charge of collection used to assemble in the Golden Temple complex from time to time to present offerings collected from their respective areas to the guru for use in various projects of community welfare.

When the Sikh chiefs captured political power in Panjab and organised themselves in the form of twelve *misls*, they all assembled at the Akal Takhat to take important decisions. They evolved consensus on important issues through the system of *gurmatta*. Decisions taken at these meetings were considered binding on all members of the community. When Ranjit Singh, one of the Sikh *misldars*, became the Maharaja of Panjab, the Golden Temple received special attention from him. Since the Golden Temple and Akal Takhat enjoyed unique reverence among the followers of Sikh faith, the British authorities, after taking control of Panjab, paid special attention to these shrines. Endowments made to the Golden Temple by Maharaja Ranjit Singh and other Sikh chiefs were not resumed by the British. Rather than controlling the management of the temple

Below: Jallianwala Bagh Memorial commemorates the sacrifice of innocent Indians killed during a firing ordered by Gen. Dyer in April 1919.

Far below: Because of its imposing building, unique architecture and academic excellence, Khalsa College, Amritsar, founded in 1892, remains the premier Sikh educational institution in Panjab.

Following page: Enthusiastic devotees on the causeway leading to the sanctum sanctorum

Page 93: A sevadar *with the traditional weapon standing outside the Darshani Deohdi*